THE BOARDWALK ALBUM

D1298944

THE BOARD

Scarboro Beach Park, 1910. "The Boardwalk."

City of Toronto Archives

WALK ALBUM

Memories of *The Beach*

by Barbaranne Boyer

Canadian Cataloguing in Publication Data

Boyer, Barbaranne, 1945—
    The boardwalk album

ISBN 0-919783-11-2

1. Toronto (Ont.) — Parks — History.
2. Amusement parks — Ontario — Toronto — History.
I. Title

FC3097.65.B69   1985 971.3'541
C85-099057-2   F1059.5.T687A21 1985

I'm sure that at some point in each of our lives we have experienced the heart-breaking loss of a dear friend or family member to cancer. The pain goes deep as we search in vain for answers which lie only through prayer and research. Therefore, all personal gains from the sale of this book will go in aid of research to the Canadian Cancer Society. In this way we will each have had a hand in contributing to the on going battle against cancer. We do know that one day cancer will be beaten.

© Barbaranne, Boyer, 1985.

Published by:
THE BOSTON MILLS PRESS
98 Main Street
Erin, Ontario NOB 1T0
(519) 833-2407

American Association
for State and Local History
Award of Merit

Winners of the
Heritage Canada
Communications Award

Design by John Denison
Cover by Fraser Sandercombe
Typeset by Lexigraf, Tottenham
Printed by Ampersand, Guelph

We wish to acknowledge the financial assistance of The Canada Council, the Ontario Arts Council and the Office of the Secretary of State.

Dedication

in memory of our Mother
Alice Patricia Boyer
and for
Elizabeth R. Reid

ACKNOWLEDGEMENTS

THE CITY OF TORONTO ARCHIVES — The James Collection of Early Canadiana.

THE METROPOLITAN TORONTO REFERENCE LIBRARY — Canadian History Department, the Baldwin Room and Old Newspaper Microfilm Department.

THE TORONTO BEACHES PUBLIC LIBRARY — Local History File. A treasure trove of newspaper clippings and manuscripts of recollections of the past which proved to be a valuable and in some cases the only source of information, together with a fascinating selection of old photographs. My thanks to Librarian Barbara Weissman.

THE WARD NINE COMMUNITY NEWS — Whose monthly edition includes articles recalling "The Way We Were" written by Mary Campbell, Barbara Myrvold, Bob Brown, Joan Latimer, B. Henderson, G. Domagala and Amy Vanderwal, just to name a few. Their stories never fail to spark the imagination or bring a smile to those who remember the "Good Old Days" in the Beach.

VICTORIA AMUSEMENT PARK, MUNRO PARK, KEW GARDENS AND SCARBORO BEACH AMUSEMENT PARK — compiled in part from the recollections of long time Beach residents: Bob Henderson, Waverly Wilson, Mary Denoon, Bob Brown, Charles Gregory and Olga M. Commins.

RON BARTER, ART & DESIGN SERVICES — who thoughtfully donated both his time and talent for the dedication page.

STARLAB PHOTOFINISHING SERVICES (BEACH) — thanks to Bill Duncan for the excellent work on short notice.

PHOTOGRAPHERS — Mr. Lu Taskey and Mr. Lee Cobourne who also donated their time to this project.

THE BALMY BEACH CANOE CLUB — Thank you for the help in locating those three special photographs.

ST. JOHN'S SCHOOL, UXBRIDGE, ONTARIO — A special thank you to Brother Francis Altimas for the old photos and a lovely afternoon.

BEACH FIREHALL #17 A1 SHIFT — Captains: Herb Penfold, Gerald Burton and Bill Mount. Larry (Barney Miller) Malone, Gord, Don, Kenny, Ted, Leonard, Kevin, Peter and Fred (chief cook and bottle washer) and my brother-in-law Ernie Yakiwchuk. Thank you all for the grand tour, the tall tales and the feelings.

To my family and friends for their enthusiasm and encouragement. My Dad and Stepmother, Andy and Vera Boyer, my children Glenn, Greggory and Bethany Reid. Auntie Nina, Janet and Gerry Sawyer, the Smiths, Mom, Dad and Granny and Jason and Amanda. My brother Michael and sister Linda.

With special thanks to my friend "World Traveller" Ron Brown, Stanley Kotick, my sister Janice and Wayne Smith.

The beach, 1913.

City of Toronto Archives

The Boardwalk.

THE BOARDWALK ALBUM
1878 — 1925

BOARDWALK . . . . the name alone has a way of sparking long-forgotten memories in each of us. It conjures up thoughts of another day, like the faded photographs in an old family album tucked away in a dusty attic.

The boardwalk holds a special place in the hearts of those who have known the beauty and tranqulity of a solitary walk along the beach in early spring, as the last fringe of ice melts from the rim of the shore. The boardwalk is the spirit of the moment and a gentle reminder of a sensitive past.

Memories are like fragile silken threads that in later years we spin into glorious golden yarns to share with those we love.

Some of my most cherished memories are those from my childhood. Growing up in the city's west end, Parkdale, was a marvelous experience for my sister Linda and I. With grand old houses, spooky back alleys, deserted tumble-down garages, and the waterfront, it was a child's paradise, to roam, discover and daydream in. Dunn Avenue, where we lived, is situated between two of Toronto's best-known and best-loved amusement parks, Sunnyside and Exhibition Park.

Each day, regardless of the season, was an adventure for us, but not always for our long-suffering parents, who were never quite prepared for the mischief their two little girls managed to get into. Newspaper clippings in the family album attest to the fact that life at the Boyers' was certainly never dull.

Local history has always fascinated me, so it seemed only natural, years later, to take an interest in the history of the Beach area, where our family moved during the construction of the Fred Gardiner Expressway in 1956.

It was while researching another project at the Beach Library that I discovered I was once again living on the fringe of three former amusement parks and pleasure gardens, all having ceased to exist long before I was born.

A year after that morning in the library, The Boardwalk Album began to take shape. The journey back was an exciting one, filled with nostalgia and a sense of urgency to recapture a little of yesterday. It has been lovingly put together for those who were there and do remember, and for those of us who wish we had been.

York Railway Station (G.T.R.), Main at Gerrard St., 1889.   *Metropolitan Toronto Library*

The Beach — A World Apart

Defining Beach boundaries can be difficult at the best of times. Old time Beachers will tell you the boundaries lie east at Victoria Park Avenue, west at Woodbine Avenue, and just north of Queen Street. Others insist the northern boundary line is Kingston Road; and there are those who claim the borderline is much broader, taking in Ashbridges Bay at Coxwell Avenue, Fallingbrook Road at the hundred steps with Gerrard Street the northern limit.

Regardless of the boundaries, Beach residents will all agree that the Beach is small-town living at its best. Unique and quite unlike any other part of Toronto, it is a small town that has somehow managed to remain just slightly apart from the great metropolis, retaining a certain air of hometown quaintness that is reflected beyond any boundary, real or imagined.

The Grand Trunk Railway (built at the village of East Toronto in 1884 and a major employer), the amusement parks which flourished between 1879 and 1925, the cottagers they brought with them, and the many taverns and inns were responsible for the development of the Beach area.

Villages which today make up the Beach were at one time considered too remote to be part of the City of Toronto. Norway Village, situated around Woodbine and Kingston Road, and Ben Lamond,

at Main Street, were often referred to as a "place in the neighbourhood" and later as a Toronto suburb. It remained that way until 1909. For many years the Beach area cut through several municipalities. From the time of the incorporation in 1834, the area from McLean Avenue north to Queen Street and continuing west, belonged to the City of Toronto, with the central section belonging to East Toronto, and the northeast corner to Midway until 1908 and Balmy Beach to the east, until 1909.

For the early travellers, Norway Village was the first town after leaving the city and passing through Leslieville, along Queen Street. One's first glimpse of the village after the last turn in the road, and over the crest of the hill along Kingston Road, was a cluster of small clapboard houses and outbuildings built haphazardly along the dirt road.

Norway boasted shops for a harnessmaker, blacksmith and wagonmaker. On the hill overlooking the Kingston Road was St. John's church and cemetery, built in 1850. East of Woodbine, a swift spring-fed creek wound its way across Woodbine Avenue and ran into Small's Pond, a little north of the present-day cemetery site. In the hollow to the east was a brewery owned by Richard Smith, whose brother James managed the Norway House on the southeast corner of Kingston Road, near Woodbine.

They were rough and tumble days along the Kingston Road, and taverns and inns were numerous along this stretch, then the main route between Toronto and Kingston. Weary travellers and bone-chilled farmers sought refuge when making the long journey to or from the city; a good place to water your team, a hot fire and a stout mug of beer could always be found.

On the northeast corner of Kingston Road and Woodbine stood the Boston House, a private hotel built in the 1870s, and opposite was the Woodruff House (also known as the Lavender Hotel), built in 1879. A little further up the road was James Shaw's hotel and stables, dating back to the 1840s. O'Sullivan's Corners, at Lee Avenue, was a popular establishment run by a dashing Irishman, one Gentleman Dan O'Sullivan, who was said to be a direct descendent of Irish royalty. A lively character, Gentleman Dan was renowned for his colourful storytelling and fine stock of liquor.

Continuing eastward was the village of Ben Lamond, situated around the Main Street area. Ben Lamond, in 1881, boasted twenty-eight residents, a scattering of farms and outbuildings, and the Victoria Hotel on the northeast corner—today it's called the Benlamond. It is commonly accepted that the village derived its name from two of its prominent citizens and large landholders, James Lamond-Smith and Benjamin Morton.

To the south of the villages, along the waterfront, early pioneers were busy building their futures. The Langs, Williams and Wilsons were among a few of the first settlers, before the peace and tranquility of the area was shattered when folks from the city "discovered" the delights of a cool summer breeze blowing in off the waters and the breathtaking views from the hills and glens, cool dark ravines and trickling creeks that wound through the tall forests.

It was during the 1850s that the boardwalk made its first appearance in the Beach. Early settlers in the Ashbridges Bay area built plank walkways between their cabins for easy access during inclement weather when the mud and water made walking difficult. Later, as the popularity of the area grew, more and more cottages began to spring up along the waterfront, and they too added boardwalks. Victoria Park, in the extreme east end, had a boardwalk which extended from the wharf into the amusement grounds. By 1907 Scarboro Beach Amusement Park had also built a promenade through the park and along the beach as an added attraction for the visitors.

Over the years, a constant battle of the elements against the boardwalk threatened to destroy a way of life residents had come to expect. In 1913 the City of Toronto appropriated $500 for necessary repairs, and again in 1929 when a severe storm hit the area, causing extensive flooding and damage along the beach. The constant damage caused by erosion and fierce storms left the boardwalk in a sad state, and for a while it seemed doomed. But a campaign which began in the 50s brought results. The residents banded together and their cry was heard loud and clear: "Save Our Beaches, Save Our Boardwalk." By 1968 new plans for development were laid out, and by 1970 people were once again enjoying the Beach promenade. Constant storms and more erosion over the years played havoc with the walk, and repairs were made again

Silver Birch Ave., looking north from Lakefront, 1912.   Metropolitan Toronto Library

Beech Avenue at Lakefront, 1885.

Metropolitan Toronto Library

Beech Avenue, 1885.   *Metropolitan Toronto Library*

Metropolitan Toronto Library

HIGH LIFE
IN TORONTO

were constructed, and a new boardwalk was built—one that could hopefully withstand the tortures of the elements.

Today the boardwalk represents a way of life, one sacredly guarded by the residents. At times they seem to resent the intrusion of outsiders, who always refer to the area as "The Beaches", but it remains as it always has, an inviting place that seems to cast a spell, a place where first-name greeting is common, a community where pride of home, school and church are still evident, and where the real pleasures of life are enjoyed.

The Beach is many things to many people: a leisurely stroll along the boardwalk after a summer rain, or gathering in the park on a Sunday afternoon to listen to a band perform, a wonderful place to recapture the magic of summers past. It is cool autumn mornings with the tantalizing aroma of freshly raked leaves and woodburning fireplaces wafting in the breeze. Snowmen and skaters and a cold blustery wind whipping in off the frozen lake. The ravines and the cool trickling creeks winding through them provide perfect spots to savour the sweet languid days of spring in the Beach.

The Beach is a family place, a summer place, fresh and alive, with quiet, shady streets and tree-lined crescents. From the grand Victorian manors, the charming turn-of-the-century cottages, and huge, rambling batten-board homes, with their towers and graceful wraparound verandahs, complete with lacy white wicker furniture invitingly placed in a way that would make Victorian ladies feel right at home— the Beach is a special place, a world away, with the charm, beauty and romance of another era.

and again, but it was clear the Beach would have to be stabilized properly before the boardwalk could be restored. Finally, the residents joined forces once again, this time with the city and Harbour Commission. Landfill was used, groynes

Mrs. Nurse's Lakefront cottage, 1912.

Beach Library

Kew Beach Bathers, 1908.

City of Toronto Archives

AMUSEMENT PARKS REMEMBERED

FOR MORE THAN half a century the amusement parks which once graced the shores along the Beach were known throughout the city, not as the greatest or the best, but simply because of the joy they brought to the thousands of visitors who made the trek east each year for a taste of the excitement and thrills offered by the parks.

It was a day when vaudeville, slapstick and melodrama ruled. Daring feats were performed daily, and laughter and tears were a part of the shows which kept them coming back year after year.

Victoria Park Pavilion, 1879.

Beach Library

VICTORIA PARK
1878 — 1912

ONCE, LONG AGO, a park was named in honour of Her Majesty Queen Victoria. This park was situated south of Queen Street, at the foot of Victoria Park Avenue, the site of the present-day R.C. Harris Water Filtration Plant. Today, one hundred and seven years later, Victoria Park has the distinction of having been one of Toronto's first public parks.

The park was once part of the property of the Blantyre Estate. Land was leased from Peter Paterson and was financed by several prominent citizens—John Irwin, Robert Davies, and P.G. Close.

The grand opening of Victoria Park was scheduled for Saturday, June 1, 1878. Leaflets were distributed and advertisements appeared in the Telegram announcing the day weeks in advance.

Expectant holidayers and picnickers flocked daily to the pier at the foot of Church Street to board the F.B. Maxwell, which ran regularly from the city to the wharf at Victoria Park.

Weighed down by picnic hampers, deck chairs and other paraphernalia, entire familes waited in long lines for the gangplank to be lowered. Once aboard, they gathered at the rails and watched as the city receded. The cooling breeze off the lake offered passengers a welcome reprieve after the stifling heat in the city. Heading eastward, they steamed past Ashbridges Bay and followed the shoreline past the villages of Norway and Ben-Lamond, high above the trees along the Kingston Road.

Excitement ran high on the decks as mothers gathered together the children, while fathers wrestled with their belongings, each jostling with other passengers to be first to view the park.

To say the least, Victoria Park was an impressive sight: built on fourteen acres of beautifully wooded land, with shady walkways and a glorious sandy beach stretching as far as the eye could see, already alive with crowds of visitors enjoying the sun and water.

The park's main feature was the rustic Grand Pavilion. Built of cedar and latticework, it was surrounded entirely by a full two-storey verandah, where Union Jacks were flown from each corner.

Along with the dance pavilion was a restaurant, where cold beer was served with a variety of sandwiches and ices. On the hill above the park at Queen Street was another attraction, the Look-out Tower. The tower rose high above the treetops and on a clear day offered visitors a breathtaking view of the lake, Scarborough Bluffs to the east, and, in the west, the City of Toronto. It was said that one could see clearly the spray from Niagara Falls. Locals nicknamed the tower "The Sway", for in high winds it could be visibly seen swaying, and in

Victoria Amusement Park, 1910. Old Picnic pavilion later used as a pumping station. Between Nursewood and Fallingbrook Roads.

Metropolitan Toronto Library

one such storm it was toppled and never replaced.

There was a small petting zoo for the children, and donkey rides. In later years, after the park was closed, these same animals were turned loose into nearby fields; this resulted in charges of cruelty brought against the park's owners. Another popular amusement was the boat ride, which featured three steampowered boats named after Christopher Columbus's famed fleet—the Nina, the Pinta and the Santa Maria.

Foot-races, with professional runners competing against the locals, were another great attraction, as were the games of chance.

Against a backdrop of cool, sparkling water, the beach and picnic grounds always seemed cool, even on the hottest days. Big old trees shaded the many footpaths that wound through the park, with tables place at intervals for picnickers.

Public figures used the park for various promotions and appearances, the most well-known being Sir John A. Macdonald, who delivered his famous six-hour speech that was transmitted by Morse code across the country.

By 1912 the popularity of the park diminished and after thirty-four years it was to be turned over to the city.

That year the Toronto Board of Education offered the city's first open-air concept summer school. The Forest School was one of three schools designed primarily for underprivileged children suffering from tuberculosis, asthma, and other health-related problems associated with overcrowded living conditions in the city.

The fresh country air was believed to be conducive to good health. So from the first of May until October, six days a week, with trolley fare provided by the Board, some two hundred children spent the summer at the Forest School, at Victoria Park on the Lake.

Until 1934 the children who attended the school

R.H. Harris Waterfiltration Plant looking North.

each summer would spend most of their time outdoors. Classes were held under the pines, but during inclement weather they retreated to a five-room building with an assembly hall that was screened in. Here, hearty lunches and dinners were served. Over the years what was generally accepted as the proper treatment and care for children with respiratory problems changed. It was now believed that the damp, chilly air was not beneficial to the continuing good health of the children, and so after twenty-two years the Victoria Park Forest School closed its doors.

During this same period the T. Eaton Company operated a boys' camp in the park. The camp provided and promoted good times, with plenty of supervised activities to keep young boys amused during their two week stay. On Friday nights the camp opened its doors to the public, and dances were once again held in the old pavilion in the park.

For fifty-six years Victoria Park, which began as an amusement park, continued to provide a service to the community, with the well-being of children in mind. Today few remember the old park at the foot of Victoria Park Avenue, or its rich history.

From a distance the low, rambling building at the foot of Victoria Park Avenue resembles an impressive architectural delight and visitors to the area are often amazed to discover that this magnificent structure is a water filtration plant.

The City of Toronto expropriated the land for a much-needed water plant during the late thirties, although it was not until after the Second World War that construction of the R.C. Harris Filtration Plant was completed.

Victoria Park would be the first of many charms on a long silver chain which would one day link the history of the Beach and the boardwalk together.

Old Wharf at Victoria Amusement Park ca 1900.   *Metropolitan Toronto Library*

Paddle wheeler "Toronto" in Eastern gap looking N.E., 1919.   *Metropolitan Toronto Library*

KEW (PLEASURE) GARDENS
1879 — 1907

IN THE GARDEN, among tall trees and late autumn blooms, stands a very special kind of cottage, a cottage built of love and time-worn stone. By the boardwalk, on the lake, it abides like a sentinel closely guarding its legacy.

In 1848 a young man named Joseph Williams came to Canada with the 2nd Battalion, Rifle Brigade. Born in London's east end in 1826, the young sergeant was destined to become one of the Beach's first pioneers.

Not long after Joseph arrived at York he met a young Irish lass at a noncommissioned officers' picnic held at the Island. They soon married, and on his bride's urging, Joseph requested a discharge from the army; life as an officer's wife did not appeal to young Jane.

On a cool, crisp morning in the spring of 1851, Joseph, Jane and their infant son left the Town of York by stage and headed for the eastern townships. That morning, as the stage rolled and bounced over the rutted road, they passed through the tollgate at Leslieville (at Lesley Street and along Queen Street). The roadway was busy with early morning traffic, various farm vehicles headed to the city with loads of firewood and livestock. Along the way, they passed spatterings of farms, taverns and inns, where weary travellers could stop, water the horses and refresh themselves before continu-ing on. Through dense forests and flowing creeks, they continued along the Kingston Road until they reached the village of Norway, situated in the present-day Woodbine Avenue and Kingston Road area. It may have been here, at the James Shaw Hotel and livery stables, that the Williams couple stopped and later left their child while they went in search of suitable farm land. Their trek through the woods eventually led them south towards the lake. There they found twenty acres of land, with fifteen acres dense woodland and the remaining five partly swamp, but with a magnificent view of Lake Ontario.

In due time land was cleared, and a cabin, which would become the first log house in the Beach, was built in 1853. This house was the first of three homes that the Williams would live in during their lifetime. The original cabin served for many years as a garage in the laneway behind a funeral home on Queen Street, and in 1960 one of the area's most significant historical sites was demolished because of lack of interest on the part of citizens.

Joseph and Jane called their property Kew Farm, and to support themselves Joseph cultivated a large vegetable garden, while his wife made home-baked goods and put down preserves and pickles to be sold weekly at the St. Lawrence Market, in the city.

Kew Beach Shelter, 1914.

City of Toronto Archives

In the pioneering spirit the young couple had a dream, and for the next twenty-five years they worked long, hard hours on the land always keeping that dream before them. Joseph named his farm (and his youngest son) after the famous Kew Gardens in London, England which had opened the year Joseph turned sixteen.

Now in his fortieth year, Joseph and his sons began clearing the land with an eye to the future. The property was heavily wooded and an economical way to transport his lumber was a major concern. The answer to the dilemma came in the form of a forty-ton vessel purchased in Port Credit for seventy-five dollars, in May 1866. With help from his sons he sailed the vessel, "Rover," eastward along Lake Ontario to the foot of their property. Lumber was in big demand in the city for fuel and building material and sold for two dollars a cord at the Wood Market on Front Street.

As the years flew by, the Williams' dream began to take shape and their plans for a pleasure garden were becoming a reality. Further east, along Queen Street, other plans were underway for the grand opening of the area's first amusement park. On June 1, 1878, Victoria Park opened its gates at the foot of the present-day Victoria Park Avenue. The summer of '78 was just the beginning of a tradition that would linger in the Beach long after the amusement parks had ceased to exist.

The following year was a jubilant one for the Williams family. In England Queen Victoria was commemorating her sixtieth Birthday, and on that same day in Toronto, May 24, 1879, Joseph Williams opened his "Kew Gardens". Flyers were circulated advertising several modes of travel by which to reach the park. One could come by street-tram to the Don Bridge, and the "very" comfortable Kingston Road Tramway; or arrive in the comfort of their own carriages, with good stabling available at the park; by rowboat, through the East Channel or Ashbridges Bay, in rough weather; then again, one could always walk, it was only a pleasant hour's journey. The park offered a variety of amusements, dancing, fishing, and "innocent" rides. Breakfast, afternoon teas and dinner could be enjoyed in the house or garden for twenty-five cents. Ladies and children were especially encouraged to visit the park, where no spiritous liquors were served.

Young Kew was seven years old that first season. With the other family members, he spent most of his childhood working in the park.

Kew Gardens proved a huge success, the park was filled with families who rented tents each weekend or stayed in one of the many cottages down along the shore for the entire season. Visitors were able to purchase fresh produce and fruit right from the garden, and catch fish anytime. The area became quite well known throughout the city as a rural resort-town, and as each year passed, more and more city folks came and built their own summer cottages—the gentry their elegant summer residences along the beach or in the gentle hills north of Queen Street.

The seasons passed, and in 1902 Kew, now twenty-three, was soon to be wed. With the help of his brothers, Kew built a magnificent home in his father's garden, with stone brought all the way from Kingston. The house featured a lovely circular staircase. A turret at one end of the house and a semicircular verandah completed the picture. During

Kew Beach looking east, 1908   *Metropolitan Toronto Library*

Sunday School Picnic, Kew Beach, 1890s.

Kew Beach at foot of Waverley Road looking towards Lee Ave. 1900s.   Ontario Archives

Kew Beach Club House, Toronto, Can.

Metropolitan Toronto Library

the next few years the young Williams couple played hosts to many friends and theatrical folks, with dinner parties and afternoon teas in the garden.

It was surely a heartbreak when, in 1907, five short years after the construction of his home, the city expropriated the land and cottages in Kew Gardens. Kew's home was spared when the public park was developed, and it serves as a gardener's home today. Kew and his family moved to another, not so grand, cottage further along the beach, but in 1925 they were forced to move once again when this land was expropriated for a different kind of park. The land included his father's original gardens, Scarboro Beach Amusement Park, and Balmy Beach to the east. The family moved to a house north of Queen Street, another heartbreak for a man who lived his life along the waterfront.

Kew Williams, his pioneering parents Joseph and Jane, and all their children would finally be remembered in the park which today bears their name, and in the lovely old cottage that sits proudly by the lake, a timeless reminder of one man's dreams.

Balmy Beach Park

Along the boardwalk, at the foot of Beech Avenue, is a clubhouse whose history dates back more than one hundred and ten years. In 1875 former Toronto Mayor Sir Adam Wilson, whose summer residence was at Balmy Beach, deeded to the Town of East Toronto land to be used thereafter as "promenade and recreation grounds." The former mayor's gift to the city would bring pleasure to thousands of Beach residents for more than a century.

It was in 1903 that a debating team, known as the Beach Success Club, made application with the officials of the recreation grounds to have their club expanded to include a clubhouse and bowling green.

Club members, made up of young men and boys, many of whom owned their own canoes were delighted two years later when the new Balmy Beach Club was officially opened. For more than eighty years members have represented the club in international competition. The walls in the clubhouse attest to the fact that indeed Balmy Beach over the years succeeded. Trophies, ribbons and faded old photographs represent their triumphs. From canoeing, rugger, hockey and volleyball the teams have been bringing home victories under the bright blue and gold banner.

Balmy Beach Club has a long, rich history, one that includes the name of a man synonymous with the Beach. He received recognition when he became a member of the Canadian Amateur Sports Hall of Fame, and a street bearing his name punctuates that Roy Nurse was regarded as one of North America's finest canoeists, a man respected and loved by fellow Torontonians.

During his brilliant career Roy Nurse won the Canadian Canoeing Championship in 1922. He held this title for ten years. In 1924 he succeeded in paddling away with three gold medals at the Paris Olympics.

Roy Nurse was born in the Beach and his death at age 81, in January 1984, was a sad loss for those who knew and loved him.

Frank Saker, Harvey Charters and Norm and Ken Lane are but a few of the former club members whose names are still referred to even today.

Balmy Beach and the clubhouse by the shore were witnesses to a grand era and few oldtime residents could forget the annual regattas held on the waterfront. Folks came from all over to watch the races and cheer on their favourites. The war canoe races at the finale were what everyone really looked forward to. Over the years a great rivalry developed between Kew Beach and Balmy Beach, and the war canoe "battles" would have crowds going wild onshore whenever a race was disputed.

Long-time resident Olga Marie Commins, recalled the two clubs' competitive spirits. "The battles were quite something to see. Yet a few years later in 1914-1918 those same boys fought together in France and many were buried far from Balmy and Kew Beach."

During the 40s and 50s the legendary dance floor at Balmy Beach was known to everyone as "the place" to go on Saturday night. Their particular style of dance, called the "balmy," was all the rage and copied throughout the city. The original clubhouse was truly reminiscent of the Golden Era. It had a boat storage at beach level and the second storey was surrounded by a railed verandah, with French doors leading onto it. Bright lanterns were strung along its length, and on balmy starlit nights couples could dance under the moonlight.

In 1963 a fire destroyed the old dance floor, but not the memories of long ago and starry nights spent waltzing with that special someone at the Balmy Beach Club.

Balmy Beach Regatta Day, 1900s.

Balmy Beach Canoe Club

Balmy Beach Park, 1907.

Metropolitan Toronto Library

Balmy Beach Club, foot of Beech Ave. 1900s.   *Metropolitan Toronto Library*

Balmy Beach Canoe Club, 1920s.

Balmy Beach Canoe Club

Balmy Beach Canoe Club, Ladies Paddling Team, 1919.

Balmy Beach Canoe Club

Munro Amusement Park, 1901. *Metropolitan Toronto Library*

MUNRO PARK AMUSEMENT PARK
1898 — 1901

MUNRO PARK WAS the second amusement park to be established in the Beach around the turn of the century. Known throughout the city as the "Trolley Park," Munro's fate was doomed from the beginning.

The Beach continued to become a popular vacation area. Countless numbers built their modest cottages, and the affluent their elaborate summer residences in the resort village. Others came for the day or stayed in canvas tents, rented by the week or season.

Because of the increasing popularity of the area, the privately owned Toronto Railway Company saw a means of increasing business by building another park along its Queen Street route. Prime land owned by the Munro family was leased to the company in 1897; it consisted of some fifty acres stretching a quarter-mile along Queen Street, with its boundaries east at present-day Nursewood Road and Silver Birch to the west. Almost immediately the T.R.C. extended their existing rails east along Queen, from Balsam Avenue directly to the park's entrance. However, not all the residents were thrilled by the prospect of another park in their midst, and on its completion the new rails were promptly removed and the tracks tossed ceremoniously into the ravine.

Ten months later, in May, the T.R.C. opened the new park and Munro proved an immediate success. On the new extended rails, visitors could ride directly to the park's entrance, which stood approximately where Munro Park Avenue is today. The trolley looped around and headed back for the city along Queen.

Situated at the entrance was a pavilion and a bicycle check where patrons could leave their bikes for five cents. Souvenirs, postcards, candy and ice cream lured visitors heading for the gates. The T.R.C. charged no entry fee but counted on the fares collected from visitors using public transportation to and from the park.

Munro Park was geared toward the family. But it wasn't unusual for bicycle clubs, which were all the rage, to choose a park for a day's outing.

Children especially enjoyed the "trolley park," donkey rides, and swings. A merry-go-round, built by Mr. Hicks from The Humber, proved very popular. Mr. Lundy's ostriches were another favourite attraction with the children, as were the swans and ducks that swam idly in the park's pond.

The Ferris wheel was the park's best feature ride. Men and boys waited eagerly in long queues, nervously nudging one another as they waited their turn, while hesitant mothers held back the small fry, declaring them too young for such a ride.

T.S.R. *Horsecar*, 1892.

Crowds of all ages were treated twice daily to Mr. McClennan and the Highlanders band. Many a lace hankie dabbed a stray tear as Mr. McClennan sang his renditions of national and patriotic songs.

By day the park rang with the laughter and shouts of delighted children, by night it was transformed into a virtual fairyland, with more than sixteen hundred coloured lights strung throughout the park—by today's standards it might appear laughable, but around the turn of the century the effect was tremendous.

Young ladies and their beaus strolled hand in hand through the garden and along the many paths leading down to the shore. The moon and stars against a midnight-blue background provided the perfect romantic effect, living forever in the memories of many.

Perhaps the best-loved entertainment provided by the park was the crowd-pleasing vaudeville show, which drew the greatest throngs. For ten cents one could secure a seat under the canopy, which also provided cover for the stage. This area was fenced in but allowed others to view the show free of charge. Families spread their blankets on the ground, while the older folks chose the comfort of canvas-covered deck chairs.

The show ran daily, Monday through Saturday, and the acts changed weekly. The Buster Brown act was a favourite, featuring the boy's famed dog, Tige. The crowds cheered loudly when the Indian Maiden, accompanied by her pony, rode on stage to sing her heart out.

During the winter months the acts which performed at Munro Park played to a packed theatre at Sheas. Many of the performers from the stage shows boarded at the several lodges in the area. One was Mr. Brown's lodge, on the northwest corner of Maple Avenue (now Scarborough Road) and Queen Street. Another was located on Balmy Avenue. the show-biz folks were, however, not all that popular with their neighbours, because of their late hours and unconventional lifestyles.

Munro Park was in its heyday as the new century began, and for all intents and purposes it had accomplished what the T.R.C. had set out to do. City folks did come and, for the most part, relied on the public transportation to get them back and forth to the city. The Beach area profited too and continued to grow.

However, disaster was inevitable. The lease on the park was coming due. The T.R.C. paid three hundred dollars per year, with an option clause of another ten-year lease, provided the rent was mutually agreed upon. In March of 1900 rumours began to circulate. It was said that Messrs. Munro, being shrewd and able to see a good thing, had sent a lease renewal to the T.R.C. stating that hence the rent would be two thousand dollars per annum.

In May 1900 the park opened on schedule with an advance advertisement appearing in the Toronto 'World' newspaper, announcing the "new attractions, new features and new improvements at Munro Park."

Spring of 1901 found the dispute between the T.R.C. and the Munro family still unresolved, and rumours flew throughout the district. The Toronto 'World' ran an article in May that heaped fuel on the fire, suggesting the T.R.C. was interested in a piece of property located east of Victoria Park— known as The Palisades, consisting of fifty-five acres of lush woodland, with a creek that ran through a shallow ravine to empty over the cliffs, forming a cascade down to the lake below.

The T.R.C. felt The Palisades would be the ideal location for a new summer resort, their trolleys would be operated on the existing line, past Munro, and continue east into the Palisades, north to the Kingston Road and to the Scarborough Electric Railway, forming a belt-line. However, this scheme was never realized.

Speculation as to the fate of Munro Park was quelled when T.R.C. officials received notice stating they were now considered trespassers. It was soon reported that there was no apparent effort taking place to clean the grounds and ready it for another season.

That summer of 1901 was a dismal one for the Beach district. No longer did happy family groups travel east for a day's outing, with picnics on the hillside overlooking the lake. No longer did the bicycle clubs of gay blades, dressed in flashy wheelman garb, ride carefree along Queen Street, calling out to one and all. And no longer did the trolleys arrive at the park's entrance with carloads of patrons.

The boardinghouses and corner groceries were hardest hit. The Beach overnight became a ghost town. Munro Park and its forerunner, Victoria Park, had left their mark in establishing the Beach as a summer place and suddenly, for many, there was nothing to return to. It would remain this way until 1907, when the third, the largest and last of the amusement parks was developed.

Scarboro Beach by night, 1920s.

Metropolitan Toronto Library

SCARBORO BEACH
AMUSEMENT PARK
1907 — 1925

FOR THOSE RESIDENTS who welcomed the closing of Munro Park in 1901, the peace and quiet that followed proved to be only a short-lived reprieve. Once again the Beach was alive and fairly hummed with expectant activity as the shops and summer hotels began preparations to welcome vacationers to the area.

One of the most popular summer hotels of the day was the Alexandra, located at 326 Lakefront just east of Balsam Avenue situated on the beach overlooking the lake. For 24 summers the three storey frame building owned and operated by Mrs. Wilson proved to be a favourite haunt for folks seeking an escape from the sweltering heat in the city. Surrounded by tall shady trees and wide railed verandahs, with a lawn that stretched down to the sand, guests could relax in comfort, canoe along the shoreline or gather for an afternoon of lawn bowling at the Balmy Beach Club. For those seeking solitude a picnic lunch provided by the hotel allowed couples and families the opportunity to venture out on their own.

It was during those early years that ladies wore ankle length skirts that barely skimmed the boardwalk, wide brimmed picture-frame hats and carried parasols they twirled with practiced ease to ward off the unbecoming suntan so admired today.

Dapper young men sporting straw boaters paused to salute those they passed, the inevitable bicycle at hand.

The year was 1907 and seemingly overnight a great park rose up, one that would be recalled many years later as one of Toronto's most memorable parks.

Scarboro Beach Amusement Park was comprised of thirty-seven acres situated east of Kew Gardens, between McLean and Leuty Avenues, the park ran south from Queen Street to the waterfront.

The Toronto Railway Company succeeded once again in increasing its ridership through the city's east end, with a larger and more exciting park awaiting visitors along its Queen Street route. Filled to capacity, the trolleys rocked and swayed along the rails, over the Don River, past the Old Woodbine Race Track and Kew Gardens; excitement rose as the tower in the park came into view, then disappeared behind a long row of stately chestnut trees lining the road. Looping in through the north east corner of the park, the trolley would discharge its passengers near the entrance gates before it continued on around the loop and back onto Queen Street. An air of festivity welcomed visitors; bright-coloured flags and pennants flew everywhere, with strings of lights outlining all the buildings. Crowds hurried towards the little booth near the gates to pay their dimes in return for a full day's worth of thrills and excitement and memories.

The tower just beyond the gates was a familiar site and quickly became a meeting place for thousands of park visitors. Surrounded by a wooden boardwalk with classic park benches at its base, the tower rose one hundred feet. By night the tower shimmered and sparkled, with more than a hundred strings of clear lights decorating its column. Set high atop was a powerful beacon whose bright light could be seen for miles around in any direction. During the early twenties a fierce windstorm struck the area and the tower surrendered to the elements, never to be replaced. The tower had become a hallmark of the park and many mourned its absence.

Scarboro Beach had a Coney Island atmosphere that prevailed along the midway, lined with concession booths offering games of chance and refreshments—the five cent red hot, ice cream, and other delectable confections. Sidewalk hawkers tantalized visitors with gaudy souvenirs amid the chaotic hustle-bustle atmosphere. Although the little ones stood in awe, eyeing everything around them, it was the spectacular rides and the open-air theatre with magicians, acrobats and jugglers that drew them like magnets.

The roller coaster was located near the entrance, and ran east and west. Riders got a topsy-turvy view of the park as the cars shot downward then up a series of hills, high above the concession booths and over the back yards of the homes on Leuty Avenue. Through a dark tunnel, with minia-ture towns lining the track, the cars swooshed up and around the curves, chased by the screams of its riders. The roller coaster ride always seemed too short as the cars pulled into the shed by the observation bridge near the "chutes."

The park's Tunnel of Love was another ride guaranteed to produce wild screams, as riders wound their way along a dark water passageway. Clinging to one another, just in case, couples shrieked in the dark as a bloody corpse fell forward, a large butcher knife embedded in its chest, accompanied by ear-splitting music from a concealed player piano. Slightly embarrassed adults and teary-eyed children staggered into the bright afternoon sunshine, a little the worse for wear.

By far the most popular ride at the park was the famous "Shoot the Chutes." After boarding little boats, riders were jerked up an incline to a covered platform high above the midway, to wait apprehensively for the ride of a lifetime. Travelling at a high speed, the boats rocketed downward seventy-five feet, passing under the spectator's bridge, through an archway, and landing with a resounding splash in the middle of the lagoon, sending a great spray of water off in all directions. Laughing and no doubt soaked, they scrambled from the boats with the sounds of whistles and cheers from onlookers on the bridge ringing in their ears.

The next stop was the "House of Fun," where spectators probably enjoyed themselves more than those who entered. Inside was a sectional bridge that caused squeals of laughter and shouts of surprise as it teetered and twisted when crossed. Upon exiting, a blast of air caused a definite flush on the faces of ladies struggling to hold down

On the midway Scarboro Beach Park, 1907.

City of Toronto Archives

47

After shooting the Chutes, 1909.   *City of Toronto Archives*

Watching the Chutes, 1908.

City of Toronto Archives

their long skirts amid gales of laughter from the gathered crowd.

Located near the "Chutes" was another popular attraction. The San Francisco Earthquake and the Johnstown Flood production drew large crowds. The earthquake scene was set up on stage with an elaborate background depicting a miniature city complete with tiny wooden buildings. Folks gathered to watch the impending disaster unfold before their very eyes. Off to the right a lecturer would reconstruct the events leading up to the catastrophe. The audience held their breath as the houselights dimmed and went out, then suddenly there was a great flash of light followed by a low rumbling, an effect produced by shaking a long piece of tin. At this point the lights came on, and there, where once neat rows of buildings had stood, was the total destruction of San Francisco, complete with all the little buildings lying on their sides in tidy disarray.

Folks who remember this stage act also recall the Johnstown Flood production was the same, except that at the end the speaker would look off into the distance and yell in a loud and horrified voice: "My God, the dam has burst." They say this act never varied, and sometimes smelling salts had to be administered to those who were badly frightened.

At the open air theatre, crowds were entertained daily by magicians and jugglers. The Strongman show, featuring brothers Art and Bill Edmond, was a favourite among the men and boys. While Art demonstrated his muscle flexing abilities, brother Bill would taunt the crowd with his offer of ten bucks to any man who could throw Art to the mat in ten minutes.

Another regular at the park was dashing Prince Nelson. During his evening show the Prince would decorate his body with strings of electric lights and delight the crowd with his dance across the highwire, causing oohs and ahhs as he dipped and swayed high above them. The act was made even more interesting by the Prince, who offered ten dollars to anyone who would ride his shoulders on the highwire. None was ever known to except his challenge.

Daring feats seemed to be the order of the day, with the various parks trying to outdo each other to draw the largest crowds of spectators.

On September 2nd, 1909, an advertisement appeared in the Toronto Star: "Willard aeroplane sails from Scarboro Beach to Niagara. To see Season's Sensation go to Scarboro Beach."

How many Torontonians remember a day on September 7th, 1900 when Foster Charles Willard became the first man to ever fly an airplane over the city of Toronto?

Foster Willard was the fourth American to ever fly, and was brought to Toronto to put on a flying exhibition. He arrived in the city on August 28th and made his first attempt to fly his "Golden Flyer" from a runway constructed at Scarboro Beach Park, which ran from between the buildings in the park out onto a pier. His first flight was a failure, with the plane landing in the lake. The following day the headline read "Airship went Up and Airship came Down." Five days later, after necessary repairs had been completed, Willard successfully flew his plane approximately two miles over the water and once again splashed into the lake because the crowds lining the shore made a beach landing

e Tower and Chutes, 1911   *Metropolitan Toronto Library*

impossible. His final attempt on September 11th ended with yet another dunking when engine trouble forced him down. Shortly afterwards Willard left for his home in New York but returned in 1911 for an airshow at Donlands Farm.

The Balloonman, who entertained with his death-defying leap, was perhaps not as exciting as the Willard air show but did manage to draw crowds just the same. From a pipe suspended from the bottom of the balloon, he would parachute to the ground below, landing with a great flourish. One such leap resulted in the gentleman having to be rescued by the Beach Volunteer Fire Brigade, after he accidentally landed in the treetops at Balsam Avenue and Queen Street. The crowds gathered and cheered as the Balloonman was brought safely down. The incident may have been a little hard to live down for a while, but it did result in a larger attendance at his shows thereafter.

In the northwest corner of the park stood the Athletic Grounds. It was here that thousands, over the years, cheered on a multitude of athletes participating in a variety of sporting events.

Endurance contests were all the rage and, from the sublime to the ridiculous, almost anything went. Park managers were always in search of something different or unusual to entice folks to their parks.

One popular spectator sport held on the Athletic Grounds was the six day bicycle race, in which participants cycled for one hundred and forty-four continuous hours, stopping only for food and drink. The popularity of the race drew top named cyclists from all corners of the globe, including two famous

51

Canadians, William "Torchy" Peden and Fred Spencer, who successfully held their title at the Six-Day Marathon at Madison Square Garden three years in a row.

Foot races held on the dirt track of the lacrosse field also included some big name professionals— Shrubbs, Durando and Tom Longboat, winner of the Boston Marathon in 1907.

As a soft summer day gave way to evening, the park was transformed into a magical place that sparkled and twinkled as the night grew darker. The bandshell gleamed under the lights, the brass instruments looked bold and shiny. A hush swept over the crowd as the bandmaster tapped his baton against the music rack—still silence—and then the glorious, exciting sound of music filled the air. Soft waves of melody filtered through the trees and washed around the park, down towards the waterfront, where young couples strolled hand in hand along the boardwalk; the music drifted across the still waters to where hundreds of canoes floated lazily offshore, their occupants content to savour the moment.

The band concerts held in the park were a treat looked forward to by thousands over the years. Italian bandleader D'Urbano delighted crowds with his own brand of music, as did Maggie Barr, whose lilting voice was said to have brought a tear to the eye of even the most hard-hearted. This Scottish lass was praised in the local papers as the "Queen of Scottish Song" and welcomed with open arms.

A black quartet called the Harmony Kings charmed visitors, as did the military bands with their drums and bugles, sending a chill up your spine as the exciting blast of music filled the air.

Afternoon and evening band concerts held in Scarboro Beach Park would be remembered by many long after the park closed its gates forever.

The concessions are boarded up. The painted signs are fading, the footpaths overgrown and the boardwalk, with its gay-coloured lights, hang limp. The stadium echoes with applause for athletes, their names long forgotten, and the bandstand in the park, once alive with the sweet strains of music, is now only a memory. In the dance pavilion the ghost of summers past make eerie shadows across the dance floor, with only the moan of the wind to disturb the silence.

It was October 25, 1925, and Scarboro Beach Park had just concluded its eighteenth season. An advertisement appeared in a Toronto newspaper, calling for tenders for the demolition of the buildings in the park. Some would say the park simply lost its appeal after the new competitor, "Sunnyside", opened its gates in the city's west end in 1922. The land was now in the hands of the Provident Investment Company, who purchased the property during a cleanup campaign in the Beach area. Blueprints showed new streets laid out where once a park had stood, and plans for the construction of hundreds of new homes were underway and scheduled for the spring of 1926.

The dismantling of Scarboro Beach was swift. One by one the concessions were bulldozed under and the amusements disappeared. Some would be sold to other parks in the province. The carousel is believed to have been sold to the Lakeside Park, in Port Dalhousie.

Listening to the band at Scarboro Beach, 1911.   *Metropolitan Toronto Library*

Aerial of Scarboro Beach, 1920s.   *Metropolitan Toronto Library*

Scarboro Beach Park, 1922.

Metropolitan Toronto Library

Most of the cottages facing the lake were expropriated by the city to make room for a new mile-long park. Cottages were sold cheaply to anyone wanting one, and some ended up in strange places. Doing double duty, one such building served as a children's playhouse for many years, another became a garage, and several were moved out of the area to become cottages once again on other lakes. Those left unwanted were simply razed.

Seven years later at the stroke of midnight on Victoria Day 1932, more than sixty thousand people gathered on the beach for a giant bonfire to celebrate the opening of a new park, appropriately named "The Beaches." One hundred and seven years have passed since the first park in the Beach opened its gates, and when the death knell tolled one final time, the people asked for and received their park along the waterfront, where future generations will laugh and play in the sunshine, unaware of the history of a boardwalk that has endured the passage of time.

Fallingbrook Estate, home of Sir Donald Mann, 1917.　　　　　*Metropolitan Toronto Library*

Fallingbrook Pavilion
and
St. John's Industrial School

At the foot of Fallingbrook Road and Queen Street is a pathway that winds haphazardly down a steep incline to the beach below. It's called "the hundred steps" and it is here that for more than half a century visitors found their way down to the pavilion built at the base of the bluffs.

In 1907, the same year Scarboro Beach Park opened, Sir Donald Mann built his fabulous estate on a large tract of land just west of the Hunt Club along Kingston Road, which he called Fallingbrook.

Meanwhile, at the foot of the bluffs below the Mann estate , a pavilion was built, complete with a boat storage, change rooms, ice cream stand and dance hall. It was known throughout the district as the "Bucket of Blood" because of the numerous fights which took place there on weekends. Nevertheless, the popularity of the pavilion continued.

Local kids, families and the boys from St. John's trooped down Victoria Park Avenue to "the hundred steps" for a swim on hot summer days. St. John's Industrial School, located south of Kingston Road on Victoria Park Avenue on the Old Bantyre Estate, was originally the property of Dr. Orlando S. Winstanley. Purchased in 1848, it consisted of fifty acres extending from Kingston Road to the lake. In 1850 the property was sold to Peter Paterson who built a sprawling two-storey mansion calling it Blantyre Park. Forty-two years later in 1892, Archbishop John Walsh bought the estate along with fifteen acres as a summer residence. The Archbishop was a man with a vision, and to this St. John's owes its beginnings. On November 16, 1895 the school's first Inaugural ceremony and open house was held.

In its rural setting, built among mature maples, manicured lawns and acres of cultivated gardens with tropical potted palms lining the circular drive, St. John's was indeed an impressive sight. Under the direction of Mr. O'Byrne, the boys were taught a trade and over the years evidence of their accomplishments could be seen throughout the school and property.

The boys who attended St. John's were a credit to the community and visitors were always impressed by the attitude of the boys towards those in authority. The Brothers who taught at the school were firm but gentle in their dealings with the students and this attitude of fair play, loyalty, discipline and the ability to get along were taught both in and out of the classroom.

Although the school has been gone for more than twenty-eight years there are those who fondly recall the early days when you went to St. John's to get fresh drinking water and vegetables while camping on the north side of Queen Street opposite

St. John's Industrial
School–gymnasium.

St. John's, Uxbridge

St. John's Industrial
School–rear view.

Munro and Victoria Parks in the summer. Others will remember the Handball Alleys built in 1907; the greenhouse and the first automobile purchased by the school in 1917; the annual fireworks and, of course, "Bosco" the school's mascot, a great dane; skating on clear, crisp winter evenings; swimming in the lake and cheering on the school's hockey, football, soccer and handball teams.

July 8, 1957 heralded the end of an era in the Beach. Sixty-three years and 4,200 boys later, St. John's Industrial School closed its doors for the last time at Blantyre Park.

it once was and with aging buildings in desperate need of attention, the decision was made. July 1957 proved to be another new beginning, not the end of St. John's.

In January 1930, a fire which started at the Mann Estate and spread to the pavilion below on the beach destroying both, left its mark and today, fifty-six years later, a sign partly hidden among overgrown trees on the path is posted as a warning of danger, and a chain bars the way to the "hundred steps" which no longer exist. All that remains of the "Bucket of Blood" are fragments of concrete

"That ole gang of mine",
St. John's Industrial School,
circa 1930s.

It was with mixed emotions that the Brothers and the boys in their care boarded buses and left for their new home in Uxbridge. Brother Francis Altimus, who was at the time Director and Superintendent, recalled their feelings as being emotionally divided. After being part of the community for seventy-four years, the Brothers and boys had formed a close relationship with their neighbours and many lifelong friendships had developed. It was truly hard to sever the ties. Over the years the village grew, it was no longer the rural community

buried in the sand and as late as the seventies the corner stone could be seen embedded on the beach amidst rotting debris, driftwood and old car tires, hardly a fitting resting place for a grand old pavilion that once rocked to the beat of dance-bands and catered to thousands of kids and families who swam and frolicked along the shoreline.

Fallingbrook Pavilion, The Hundred Steps and St. John's Industrial School left behind them precious memories that are an integral part of our boardwalk history.

Old Woodbine Racetrack, 1924.   *Metropolitan Toronto Library*

THE OLD WOODBINE
1874 — 1956

"THEY'RE AT THE post—they're off." For more than one hundred and twelve years Torontonians have thrilled at the call to the post, a call synonymous with racing around the globe.

Considered one of the finest tracks in Canada, Greenwood abounds with history, enriched by the pounding of a million hooves. Situated on Queen Street, between Coxwell and Woodbine Avenues, and bordering the lake in the city's east end, Greenwood is one of the few tracks where patrons take a streetcar to the main entrance. Opened in 1874, it was originally called the Woodbine Riding and Driving Park. Seven years after it opened, the grandstand was razed by fire and rebuilt in 1881, when the Ontario Jockey Club was formed. For more than half a century Old Woodbine was the illustrious home of the Queen's Plate. From 1863 to 1883 various towns and cities throughout Ontario hosted the running of the Plate, until the Governor General, the Marquis of Lorne, urged Queen Victoria to legislate that the Queen's Plate never again be held outside the City of Toronto.

The Plate holds the honour of being the oldest uninterrupted stakes race in North American history.

Prior to this decree, the race was once held at the New Market Race Track, located behind Gates Hotel, at Danforth and Westlake Avenues. The inn, built in the 1850s by hosteler Charley Gates, a man renowned in the district for his knowledge of "good horseflesh," was a popular track, known throughout the city. After his death, the hotel and track were purchased by William Owen and called the BayView in the 80s. When Woodbine opened in 1874, the New Market track gradually failed, and finally closed around the turn of the century.

Over the years, Woodbine underwent many changes. In 1956 a new Woodbine was built in the city's northwest Malton area and the old track was renamed Greenwood. Although thirty years have passed, many old-time beachers and race patrons still refer to it as Old Woodbine.

During its seventy-two year history, Woodbine played host to royalty and dignitaries, who came to witness the running for the Plate. Northern Dancer, Secretariat, and numerous other famous horses have had the honour of running the turf at historical Old Woodbine Race Track in the Beaches.

Beach Firehall,
Queen St. E.
at Hubert
Ave. 1952.

Metropolitan
Toronto Library

The Firehall

The erection of a new firehall was always a welcome addition to any community, and so it was with the Beach. The first hall was a small two-storey building located near the present-day memorial fountain in Kew Gardens, and was manned by volunteers. The second was situated a little north of Queen Street, on Spruce Hill Road. During its prime the one-room clapboard station, with its humble hose and bell tower, faithfully served the neighbourhood with two hand-drawn engines, ladders and coils of hose, until the new fire station #17 was built on Queen Street in 1906. Having outlived its usefulness to a rapidly growing community, #2 hall would stand for a number of years, a silent testimony to the past. Some old-time residents can still vividly recall a day in 1910 when the old bell tolled continually throughout the day to mark the passing of King Edward VII.

Near the corner of Woodbine Avenue and Queen stands a gracious three-storey brick building with an impressive clock and hose tower. For both the fire department and the citizens of the Beach, the completion of the new hall was a memorable day. Everyone turned out to tour the new facilities and marvel at the brand-new "Waterous Firefighter" and the two chestnut horses bought to draw it. In the days before motorized vehicles, horses played a major role in firefighting. They were the pride of their stations, well-groomed and lovingly called by pet names. Their daily ritual of exercising was an event in the neighbourhood, and folks came regularly to enjoy the sight of the horses being put through their paces at the rear of the station. With the appearance of the new motorized firetrucks in the 20s, the men were sorely torn between their desire for any new piece of equipment that would benefit the community and the knowledge that it also meant the retirement of an old and trusted friend. There were many tears shed at #17 when the last of the firehorses, who had provided long and honourable service, were farmed out. The Beach hall would be one of the last in the city to use horse-drawn vehicles (1931).

Gone now are the days of the volunteer fire-fighters and the Bucket Brigade with their hand-drawn engines, at #17 the past lingers on, from the polished brass pole rising a full two storeys, to the old wall-mounted fire bell. But, it's in the tower that the past really comes alive. The men jokingly tell you it's haunted, perhaps it is. On the third floor landing a key is used for access to the clock tower door. From here you climb a narrow flight of stairs that creak and groan with each step you take. In the dimness you find a old ladder attached to the wall and you climb, without looking down, high up into the tower. Eight small windows surround the wall, and the remnants of the original clock lay scattered about, their working parts long since removed. You take notes and marvel at the views; one can imagine the steeple of old St. John's to the north, it's bell tolling the hour; to the east the tower at Scarboro Beach Park, the midway crowded with throngs of happy people; and to the southwest the never-ending expanse of sparkling waters, alive with steamers and pleasure crafts making for the wharfs along the shore.

A sudden chilliness in the air makes you shiver, you turn half expecting to find someone behind you, but no one's there.

The year is 1918. A cooling summer breeze filters in through the open windows, drying the hose hung the night before, the muffled sounds of voices and laughter drifts up from the street, where several men lounge in the open doorway of the hall, enjoying the late afternoon sun. Off in the distance the steady clip-clop of hoofs and the clatter of wagons rolling along the street, mingle simultaneously with the sights and sounds of another day.

The unmistakable sound of a key turning in a lock and the creaking of old wood echoes through the tower. A sandy head emerges, then the broad shoulders encased in a uniform reminiscent of another time, its brass buttons gleaming in the fading light. He climbs up on the plank floor and methodically begins to close each window, pausing to latch each one carefully. At the last one he hesitates. It is that time of day—just before dusk, just before nightfall—when all the world seems at peace. Thoughtfully he turns towards the ladder, draws his hand across his handlebar mustache, then quickly takes a small penknife from his jacket and carefully carves his initials and the date in the centre beam that rises into the gloomy reaches of the tower. He is gone as quickly and silently as he came, with the last golden rays of daylight streaking across the darkening sky.

More than a century has passed and many men have climbed to the tower and left their marks there, a fitting legacy that endures the passing of time and remembers the men who risked their lives for the prevention of fire and the preservation of life; those heroes who have gone on.

Malvern Brass Band, ca 1900.

Metropolitan Toronto Library

England's Candy Shoppe, 1054 Queen St., 1900.

Beach Library

Another Era

FROM THE END of October until the first of May each year, the Beach reverted to a sleepy village. Shopkeepers, boardinghouse owners and local residents all breathed sighs of relief as they watched with amused interest the last of the summer folk depart at the season's end. Aboard carriages piled high with trunks and hampers, families laughed and waved and bade their final farewells with promises to return next summer. Under a hazy autumn sky, the Beach regulars settled back once again into a regular pattern they would follow until winter gave way to spring.

During the winter months blustery winds whipped through the skeletal limbs of the maples and the snow lay deep, curls of smoke drifted up from the chimneys of cottages, nestled snugly behind lilac hedges, and along the boardwalk rows of boat-houses, secured for the winter, cringed at the onslaught of bitter winds and icy waves that lashed the beaches. The concessions on the midway and the bandstand in the park lay silent under a thick blanket of snow, while the residents went about their daily routines. High drifts rose above the roads and pedestrians expertly dodged the wooden tramcars of the Toronto Railway Company and the cutters that dominated Queen Street. Around the turn of the century, automobiles were still much of a novelty and few Torontonians could afford them. Tradesmen serviced the area, selling firewood, milk and bread, winding their way up and down the ice-covered streets, past the elegant summer homes of the city's affluent, interspersed with the more modest dwellings of the working class. Mock-Tudor and Edwardian stucco houses, with steep slate roofs, and stately country manors, with their elegant bowed windows, rubbed elbows with grand Victorian mansions, surrounded by their gracious wraparound verandahs, towers and turrets, and beautiful stained-glass doors. Dainty New England-style cottages, adorned with yards of delightful gingerbread, sat demurely behind white picket fences; ornate gazebos, in park-like settings, suggested days of quiet, elegant Victorian charm, with all the romance and tranquility of the more golden moments few of us remember. Those earlier years, however, were not all that rosy or carefree for most. For many of our pioneering grandparents, life began on the other side of the world, and each came with their own private dreams. Thousands of immigrants suffered untold miseries and hardships, crammed into any vessel deemed fit to sail to the New World. But any heartache or anguish endured was like a grain of salt in the wind compared to their dreams of a new beginning. And so they came: the hardy Scots, the English, and the spirited Irish. They were industrious and hardworking, and carved a place for themselves in Canadian history. Each park and pleasure garden along the silver shores of the lake represents a very special charm that links our heritage together. The lasting memories left behind are a legacy to be guarded and treasured, a reminder of a unique past and the people who pioneered in the Beach. And still there are no historical plaques to mark their sites.

Victoria Park   1878 — 1912
Kew Pleasure Gardens   1879 — 1907
Munro Park   1898 — 1901
Scarboro Beach Park   1907 — 1925

The parks have all gone now but their legend lives on.

Maude Anderson of Waverley Road with visiting relatives, 1911.

Beach Library

Kingston Road home.

Beach Library

127 Wheeler Avenue, 1923.

Department of Public Works

Corner of Balsam and Pine.

Corner of Pine and Beech Ave.

The "Hundred Steps."

#1 Fallingbrook Rd., near the "Hundred Steps."